About the Author

Elizabeth Green is a university student in Utah. She is working towards a bachelor's degree in Anthropology. In her spare time, she continues to write poetry. She is committed in her attempts to contact the Utah legislature to create new internet laws that will protect minors online.

Seven Years of Silence

Elizabeth Ann Green

Seven Years of Silence

Vanguard Press

VANGUARD PAPERBACK

© Copyright 2023
Elizabeth Ann Green

A CIP catalogue record for this title is
available from the British Library.

ISBN 978 1 83794 028 8

Vanguard Press is an imprint of
Pegasus Elliot Mackenzie Publishers Ltd.
www.pegasuspublishers.com

First Published in 2023

Vanguard Press
Sheraton House Castle Park
Cambridge England

Printed & Bound in Great Britain

Dedicated to Cathleen, who believed in who I could
become before I could see it myself

Contents

Preface

My name is Elizabeth Green. I was born in July of 1999, and at the time of writing this I am twenty-two years old. When I was fifteen years old, I became trapped in a toxic relationship with a forty-two-year-old pedophile. For over a year, he controlled nearly everything I did. This man decided who I spoke to, what I wore to school, and most importantly, where I was always. He spoke of deranged sexual fantasies that he wanted to perform on, with, and to me. He effectively took over my life from the convenience of his cell phone. This predator had me thoroughly convinced that one day I would move to California and become his wife; I just needed to graduate high school. I would become the mother to his two children who were between the ages of eight and ten years old at the time of our correspondence. I will not give their names out of respect to their privacy.

From the moment of meeting my abuser online, to our year-long interaction, the six years of waiting for any criminal justice investigative action that would lead to arresting this man and the year it took to reach a conviction, I have changed significantly. I had spent seven years in silence. I am no longer the chronically ill teenager who was at one point desperate enough for attention that I would willingly allow a pedophile to degrade me daily.

I have compiled a selection of poems that I have written about my experiences while interacting with this predator. This book is intended to showcase the emotional and physical trauma I have experienced at the hands of a cruel, manipulative man, the psychological damage I received while trying to balance adolescence with a secret life of abuse, and the painfully slow process of trying to piece together my identity when its pieces have been so terribly warped during the formative years of my life. Of course, no one ever tells the entire story. This publication could never document my entire experience, but through glances into my thoughts and emotions, I hope that I can bring awareness to the often dismissed or avoided issue of child grooming. I hope that other survivors can find validation and comfort in knowing that they are not alone in their experiences or struggles.

The Beginning

I was old, older than a child should be at that age.
Old enough to know that happily ever after isn't guaranteed
To know my illnesses will continue to worsen
And whatever is destroying my digestive system is destroying my parents' love for one another.
Old enough to recognize that the boy from church with disheveled hair who once played a song for me on his cello doesn't meet my gaze in the hall anymore, while my hair stops growing and my fingernails splinter
Old enough to know why the beautiful girls stood together in circles, pressed against each other's shoulders.

A locked gate I was not invited to enter.

But I was young, too.
Too young to know how to talk to boys
Old enough to notice that the girls my age were wearing mascara and lip-gloss to look sexy
Too young to know what sex was.
That's when he found me.

Rather, I found him. I found him the way an unlucky fish finds the hook that will pierce through her eye and leave her suffocating on a boat's blood-stained floor.

A notification lit up the darkness of my bedroom,
A man
Telling me I was beautiful, smart, mature. But more than that,
He told me I was sexy.
His syrupy sweet words washed over my taste buds like the first bite of pancakes on a Sunday morning.
I was reborn overnight. I wasn't just a wilting adolescent anymore
I was sexy.

When he messaged me I felt as light as a feather.
Compliments as bold and red as the blood filling the vials from the IV a phlebotomist taped to my arm.
I had found comfort and understanding from a perceived – albeit peculiar – peer. All that was required from me was the entirety of my attention and the promise of confidentiality.
I had an alternative life in my pocket
A secret to fill the gaps in my solitude and silent sorrow
I gave him my kindness, my innocence, and submission.
He showered me in praise when I revealed I was a virgin.
He was the sweetest poison I ever drank.
I never noticed the monster's spider-like limbs.
Softly luring me further into his web.

I wanted so badly to be perceived as an adult
I already lived in a house of cards that could fall apart at
any given moment
I thought that this man and I could move into a snow globe.
Become a delicate ornament, trapped in time and glitter,
yet onlookers who spared a glance would say I was pretty.
I played house with the monster under my bed.
When he spoke of taking my virginity, I made the fatal
mistake of trying to flirt with an Apex Predator.

"Why take my virginity when I could just give it to you?"

I had just struck myself in the heart with an icicle,
The perfect murder weapon, as it melts into nothing over
time.
Later, people will question whether there was a weapon at
all.
Ice is generally perceived as cold,
When one is exposed to its surface long enough, it burns
and scars
I was suffocating in his grasp.
I was no longer beautiful, smart, or mature
I was a slab of meat with a discount sticker slapped onto
the side.

He spoke of fantasies that would make convicts flinch.
The bastardized ways he wished to cut me:

Along the nostril, the crease of my smile, my areola, my collarbone, along the curve of my neck, teasing my jugular.

His wish was to shove a blade inside of me between my legs, to make sure I was wet enough to

Take him.

If I didn't behave I could end up like a bird served on a Christmas platter

After a weak ejaculation he would fumble around and switch his mask to the one lying on his nightstand and shower me in praise.

How could such a sweet, thoughtful girl exist? He must be the luckiest man in the world. And if I were to take a picture of myself without the weak defense of a shirt, that would make him happy.

Don't I want to make him happy?

So happy that he wouldn't need to brush his thumb up against the breast of the girl in a wheelchair he cares for at work.

But I could confide in him, tell him about my day in earnest in a way I could never speak to my parents,

And the creature would at least pretend to listen.

We spoke about comic book characters and podcasts, goals for the future.

He assured me that he would gladly wait three years so that he could marry me, and I could become The Stepmother to his children.

He stroked himself to the idea of impregnating me

The thought that my still developing body would lactate was enough to satisfy him and send pictures of the aftermath of his lust.

I was expected to praise him for finding me attractive enough to reach completion.
He told me that we decided I would apply for a university that was only an hour's drive away from his dwelling.
If my mother can sleep in the same bed as my father after a day of being screamed at and threatened with desertion,
Surely, I could deal with the minuscule ups and downs of being with a man who had a demented sexual imagination.

He would tell me what I liked.
He told me I liked him and his tattoos. I would like being wasted and to serve as a personal blowup doll; I'd like it if he carved his initials into my ass, so everyone knew who I belonged to.
I didn't know who I belonged to; I didn't know who I was.
I wasn't old enough to drive. I still wore braces.
Months passed by in a rhythmic pattern. I was getting used to the coin toss behavior of the man who insisted I refer to him as Daddy.
He wanted to stick needles in me like a pin cushion,
Which makes sense because I was soft and malleable, and eager to be whatever shape he desired.
He professed his love for me on a near bi-hourly basis and demanded that I say it back.

Is this not what love is? Spending time with the person who defiles then rewards you.

Pictures and text messages turned into Skype calls and performances.
I didn't have a dollar to my name, so I stole a pacifier from Walmart for his satisfaction.
Pigtails were preferred, as was a towel to lay atop my duvet in case the degenerate wished to see me relieve myself.

I grew back into my stutter.

I answered perverted text messages whilst walking to the room of my next scheduled debate. I sent illegal explicit photographs while I brushed my teeth in the morning.
At night I stared out the window and listened to the sound of rhythmic heavy breathing, faint slapping noises and the fantasies this creature longed to perform on a nonverbal autistic student. Who would she tell?
I'm his perfect doll, I would never tell.
I wondered how much it could possibly hurt to be run over by a truck.
I already felt as if my organs were on display, my body was public property.
I was a child wondering which one would be better: a lobotomy or an autopsy.
I ate my cereal and never told anyone how a man two states away wanted me to perform fellatio on him for my breakfast.

My back started spasming during class time. I would never tell the reason as to why my body was decaying. It seems that while my lips could keep a secret, my physique could not.

I sat alone at the table adjacent to the debate kids. I never told anyone that the monster dreamt of using a child's hand on his genitals.

I brushed my hair that was growing more brittle and thinner by the day.

I grabbed my binders without anyone knowing that I didn't sleep last night because the creature spoke to me for three and a half hours about how he would love to see me on my knees, sucking on his Gun, without knowing if there was ammunition inside of it.

He laughed at the thought of pulling the trigger.

I smiled on stage to receive my 1st place trophy and have my picture taken

Knowing that if the monster found out he would tell me to insert the trophy into myself and take a picture, and I would have tried. I lied that night and said I didn't win.

I carried on this revolting affair for over a year.

If I could save even one child from this man by listening to his perversions and entertaining his fantasies, I would gladly take that bullet and lie flat on my back in Hell the way I do on my mattress in my bedroom.

At least there was the promise of warmth and company.

I decided that taking all my antidepressants at once and falling into an eternal state of slumber would be easier than carrying on this existence.

My actions were interrupted by an unplanned interlude in my parents' arguing

My mother saw me swallow the last of the pills and screamed as I threw the plastic bottle on the tiles.

At the emergency room, my sobbing mother checked me in while my father sat in the chair next to mine and stared at the wall.

Among the radio static buzzing in my ears, my father placed his hand on my shoulder, forcing

Me to face him, and told me

To try harder next time.

I drank a mixture of fluid containing charcoal.

I was surveyed until midnight.

I was driven home in silence.

I entered the room where my darkest hours were spent and stared at my blank wall for two days.

I was grounded for trying to kill myself.

In the darkness I was still allotted my phone.

With every ounce of strength in my aching body, I accomplished what I had not yet been able to in my lifetime.

I said No.

I cut all contact with the parasite and erased his presence from my phone

I wasn't proud of myself for ending my torture

I didn't cry

I wasn't sad

I wasn't me.

I wore a reversible sweater the day I was pulled out of my forensics class. I was to report to the school's Office immediately. The stick-thin cheerleader who was sent to collect me gave me a snide look as I crouched down in the hallway to re-tie my Converse. As if I were wasting her class period of acting as a pseudo-secretary.

I arrived at the office with a calm and pleasant demeanor. I had just returned home from a debate trip to California where the vice-principal had come along.

Calm and pleasant abandoned ship as soon as I was asked to take a seat in a room surrounded by Administrators and police officers. Each sporting a grimace more intense than the last. Still, I was cautiously casual. They couldn't read my mind, and they didn't know me beyond the trophies I had earned for the school.

In this desert-dry room, I told myself that I was most likely selected to review the witness statement I had given when a debate member had gotten into a fight and got his ass kicked.

It wasn't until a folded piece of parchment slid across the dark, wooden, glossy desk that I felt my shoulders start to bunch and my ankles cross.

I was asked to read aloud a document that caused my stomach to twist and my hands to shake. My voice cracked the way my male peers did as I articulated cryptic sentences that twisted inside me like the wires shown inside a Hollywood-crafted bomb.

I was asked what the letter meant.

I was asked to lie upon an operating table, make the incision myself and spill my guts.

I confessed that this letter was the product of pedophilia, abuse, and stalking. I bit my lip to prevent myself from blurting out that I was just as guilty, that I had told the degenerate everything about my unsatisfactory life and my punishment was an eternity of vivid, abhorrent images and sounds haunting my mind during every hour of consciousness.

Staying up for days on end, staring out my window in the dark, and gripping a plastic pipe in fear that the monster who could send letters to my school could enter my bedroom window.

I was instructed to sit in the vice-principal's seat as I dialed my mother. I pressed the keys thinking that I might as well be signing my death certificate.

The embarrassment and horror I felt that day have seeped into my bones, marrow laced with paranoia and the inherent shame of being victimized.

Fear and guilt intertwined into the double helix that now composes my DNA. My mother was frozen when she arrived at the school, her lips trembled, her eyes watery.

I watched as a detective informed her of the events
I was too cowardly to report.
The rest of the week, I did not attend school.
I was taken to a room that was entirely beige. Flickering fluorescents highlighted the powdery foundation I had dabbed onto my face to change my complexion from a sickly green to an acceptable ghostly pale. I sat across from the detective, who was fiddling with a stack of papers. He repeated a rehearsed Statement that flew past my head like the BB gun pellet the stranger fantasized about shooting into my thigh.

I recalled the last year and a half of my life to a man who was meant to question and verify every fact I stated. I stood, hands tied behind a stake, and this man was deciding whether to spark a match.

After a recorded testimony and the confiscation of my phone, I left the office of abused children with a donated blanket. The fleece was already coarse, scattered safari animals adorning the fabric. I felt hollow.

I was a child.

I was a child who was given a children's blanket and sat in the receptionist's office between a girl no older than eight and a boy who triumphantly showed me his teddy bear and paper scribbled on with a broken crayon. Reality burst through my bleak and weary vision like Technicolor. These children had witnessed or were participants in horrors beyond my imagination, and they smiled happily. Waiting for their turn to be interviewed by an overworked detective who could offer nothing but fleece for Spilt Blood.

I was old, old enough to know about stranger danger. Old enough to know that three days into conversing with the monster, I was nothing, but an insect trapped in a Mason jar, with just enough holes poked into the lid so I could breathe

Occasionally being treated to a drop of sugar water. But I was young, young enough to hope for a conclusion. Young enough to think that stepping on glass shards myself would be enough to save another girl from the blood and scars this creature delighted in creating.

My mother asked God to make me a leader. She whispered this prayer to her maker while I was in my infancy

I look back at photographs of myself as a child and only see a potential victim who was lucky enough to not have been preyed upon. I glance over my teenage years and see not a smile, but skin that was lucky not to have been cut, quirked up against brittle bleached teeth.

I see blue eyes with discolored skin under my orbital bones
I see a weary body and precise silver lines adorning my wrists and upper thighs
I see a girl who went to war in silence and now flinches in the presence of normalcy.

I now knew there are thousands of victims hidden amongst Self-medicators, Honor Students, Dropouts, and Track and Field stars.
I attend my sister's band concert and know that at least one of these children on stage has suffered at the hands of a trusted adult. The nightmares are still present and shake me to the core. I had my father install a lock on my door that can only be locked from inside the room
I place a plastic pipe in my window so it can never open more than five inches
So, no one can reach me.
I avoid the gaze of Men, in supermarkets, gas stations, during college lectures.

I stare at the artificial stars scattered across the ceiling and ask, if I lie in bed for long enough, will anyone notice my absence?

After living a quarter of my life in shame and fear, I have come across a realization that almost feels like salvation:

I'm not even his type anymore. I am no longer a scared, desperate young girl who can easily be controlled under the promise of love and attention.

I have turned into the bastard's worst nightmare.

A woman.

A woman who recognizes her abuser.

A woman with a voice.

I refuse to be silent about my misery, a privilege not afforded to most women.

I may never see my day in court.

If he still walks down the street, then I will dance freely in the park. I will shout my freedom until my throat is strained and unable to continue.

If he sleeps easily at night, then I will create a revolution with the chants of men, women, and children so loud and deafening he will never know comfort again.

The cockroach will not be able to enter a grocery store without every patron in the building being able to view the scarlet letter inked upon his skin.

I will not allow one more child to have their innocence stolen by this twisted creature with false intentions. I demand my campaign for justice flow like blood down the streets until his hands are coated in the undeniable reality that he is nothing.

Nothing that can stop me, even if he did break me.

The pain will always stay. It will always persist. But there are things, sounds, actions, and people who will spark joy inside myself. Pain will never fade the way some people like to think.

Time simply allows the sunlight to creep in little by little and will fill the spaces in my rib cage until it feels comfortable to breathe again.

My mother asked God to make me a leader.

My time has just begun.

A Star Was Born

The first time I felt the lights shine upon me, I was unprepared.
Terrified.
Knees trembling.

I didn't know I was the headlining act.
I didn't know my lines or how I managed to fumble my way onto the stage.
All I saw were their stares.
Haunting eyes peering into my own, awaiting my next move.

The second time I knew it was coming.
I had a moment to prepare.
Makeup smeared, powdered, caked onto my body.
I almost looked like a woman.
Then the lights.

Sweat racing down my neck as I twirled and leapt and spun my sadistic story with a scarlet ribbon.
A standing ovation.
They loved me. At least, they loved the performance.

I could still make out the stares among the roses being thrown.

As I grew old, so did my performance.
The same dance
Same tears
Same story
Same stares, less now with each delivery.
This is the same act that millions of girls perform, so what made mine special?

Still, I was not ready to give up the lights.
I twirled and leapt and spun my story
Spinning on my toes until blood seeped through my slippers and stained the stage.
The muscles in my back convulsing,
The seam of my costume ripping at the shoulder,
My mind screaming at me to smile, smile, smile.

Bending towards the audience that wants to see just how far I can stretch before I snap in half.
I finish.
Sparse applause that feels like pity
I raise up my head to count the stares
Panting, I realize nobody's there.

I can never forget my last night under the lights.
A declaration of resignation had accumulated one last audience.

Tonight, there would be no twirling or leaping or spinning to be seen.
No longer are people
Interested in my recitation.
I will simply conclude my career by showing the girl behind the makeup,
Behind the costume,
Beneath the lights.

Stepping forward, gasps of horror fill the room.
Some people faint while others grow pale.
They were unprepared.
Terrified.
Knees trembling.
Stares averted.

It is one thing to view the reenactment of an appalling tale, but to lay witness to its consequences is damning.

When the monster chose me as his prey,
I attempted to escape his vise-like grip with flattery.
That false adulation went straight to his head and justified chopping off mine.

I drag my feet across the stage.
Body on full display, save seven vertebrae and a skull.
Shoulders slumped as I limp onto my mark. Limbs discombobulated and numb. Perhaps this is a blessing.
I cannot see the horror painted on my audience's faces.

I do not hear the shrieks and sobs.

It is only after the screaming subsides that the lights flicker off for good.

Bird Bones

I would love to walk alone in the forest
In solitude
There is no expectation of conversation
I practice cordiality with the plump birds perched on frail
boughs.

I took a vacation from being myself when I was fifteen
years old,
Now I pinch my thigh and feel
A woman's skin

I am not ready to be a mother

How do I care for the woman I have
Discovered without abandoning the child cowering behind
her?
The child digs crescent moons into my wrist with her
python grip
She demands food and shelter while vehemently rejecting
both

I cannot support her weight on my aching bones

The resources I scavenge are not adequate sustenance
Food riddled with maggots
A crooked shelter supported with branches whose budding
blossoms shake in the twilight
I will keep my eyes open until sunrise to protect her

I am not ready to be a woman

I spare a glance at the creature staring back at me
A stranger who mimics my actions so perfectly
A body covered in
Scars and fat and muscle,
I cannot love something so utterly flawed
And human

After days spent in isolation, I will succumb to the
inevitable embrace of slumber and
I will emerge once again,
An emotional vagabond

While I sit staring at the withered leaves
Scattered across the earth like a lover's caress
I see the reality

The woman and child

Fingers intertwined,
Laying frozen on the ground
Flesh eroded to expose a permanent grin

Truth flashes across my eyelids
Almost as bright as the lightning streaking last night's sky
Drips from my wrist like liquid scarlet

I lie down on the soft, forgiving soil
Huddling the child close to my ribs
Replacing the space between the woman's fingers with my
own
If I close my eyes for a moment, snowfall will provide us
with a posthumous blanket

Melting snowflakes give way to pollination
If I stay still for long enough, sweet budding flowers will
sprout from my lips and
Weary woodland creatures might rest upon my stomach

I have always been fond of birds.

Hate House

There is a house along my road, nestled in suburbia.
Its greatest power resides in unremarkable exterior.
Beige and brick and boring.
No one would spare a second look at the rambler standing
in a yard of domestic bliss,
No one could call it conspicuous.

There is a house along my road that holds a public secret.
Within this house lived a family; their greatest power
resided in their unremarkable behavior.

People like to mind their own business.
It's not their question to ask,
Not their child to raise,
Not their family to maintain,
And so, the house remained.

There is a house along my road that holds heaps of hatred.
Within this family there was a child
Sweet and isolated.
The new Stepmother harbored evil so deeply concentrated,
That when abusing her new stepdaughter,

The Father and Brothers aided.

Powder-white skin turned purple with force,
Everything went to hell during the divorce
So, the coward Husband's voice'd gone mute
When his daughter was viciously beaten by this brute.

There is a house along my road that held a body, ten years old,
Upright despite the lack of life inside her.
The linen closet was just the place
To shove an angel when the disgraced bitch was done tormenting the poor child for the day.

People like to mind their own business,
But when police cars arrive and they swarm a residence,
An audience can start to form down the street.

The news story began when the ambulance came, and
After a while of playing the waiting game,
Paramedics rolled out a small body covered on a white sheet.

There is a house along my road; the family inside had decided to move, as half of them would now be wearing stripes.
The house remains and so does pain, but I swallow it when passing by because

I remind myself the house has been empty for almost half my life.

There is a house along my road where a fire started and took life where life had been taken.
I forgot to breathe when hearing the information.
Ashes to ashes, let the house fry.
Let it serve as a reminder why evil can always find its way underground.

There is a house along my road that was rebuilt.
Now up to code, the house is looking like it should be sold quite soon.

There is a house along my road; I pass by and see a sign that hadn't previously been in the windowpane.
It has stars bordering a large tacky font that promises to Make America Great Again.

My heart skips a beat. Looking at my feet, my vision reeled.
I take a shaky breath and know that I won't forget that
Within this house a girl was killed.

There is a house along my road,
That once burnt down and now is sold to a person who supports the slimy excuse for a man that places children in cages.

A child in a cage or a child in a closet,
Who hears their screams as adults line their pockets?
Realtors and Presidents alike.

There is a house along my road
Rebranded once again to fit into suburbia.
Its greatest power resides in the fact that
Hate will ensure its continued existence.
Its cancerous hate is one that can't be escaped
And it gathers support from a distance.

A Never Has Been

I triple check the words I've clumsily laid out in front of
myself
Using a thesaurus to remove, to improve and
Replace the thoughts I originally composed.

Everything needs to be perfect, to be poised and precise
I want my words to glide through the eye of an impossibly
thin needle effortlessly.

I beg myself to create, and that it be immaculate upon
conception
To make up for the fact that it's me writing these words.

Me

Someone so lost in the river of young potential that I fear
I'll drift off into a shallow stream of hypotheticals
If I can't produce something and watch the little hand on
Life's wristwatch freeze for a beat while I submit my
offering of
Fragmented sentences and hastily smoothed-over verse.

I see pride in my mother's eyes, and I feel the need to break contact
I must have fooled her into thinking I was marvelous the way I have fooled others

For now, I allow my vision to remain unfocused
Facing my whiteboard and waiting for a muse that may never arrive.
An innovation to justify my existence in this world.
The rent I am so eager to pay for taking up space that could have been given to someone else.

Until that time, when inspiration electrifies my consciousness, I can offer only myself.

If only I were enough to satisfy my own hunger.

Forceful

After reaching one year of age, the world expects a baby to blather.
Nonsensical noises act as a window into their emotions; if a word were to form, all the better.

Growing further, at four or five, a child should know how to scribble a line that resembles the characters used to spell their name.

Progressing in age, different milestones are placed, all with the intention of watching the child succeed.

So, I can say with proud certainty that by the age of eleven I was Forceful.

Other children my age were showered with praise and descriptors far different from mine.
Artistic and Kind stood at the front of the line where Forceful trailed near the end,
Creating fantasy worlds with Energetic and Distracted where Forceful could choose any role and play pretend.

Time continued to pass and while I aged alongside my class, Forceful was taken away.

I kept level ground with grown men and wouldn't concede to jests made in poor taste
So Forceful was gone and Snarky had taken her place.

Snarky was not as favored as Ambitious or Opinionated, the only difference between them their perceived sex.

How different the world would be if adjectives were not purchased with gendered currency.

Wildfire

I hate that I do this.
I'm just a fragile pile of kindling,
And I trick myself into believing that I'm glowing.
I don't smell the smoke rising,
When my eyes start to water I tell myself
It's because I'm growing.
And I am

I'm sucking in the air around me and expanding.
Emerging into a fully formed flame before I notice
something's off.
I become too restless to cope.

The five things I can see are all flammable and now the
stuffed
Easter bunny's melting at my touch.
Plastic eyes dribbling down the torched body I tried to save
To save myself
One ear falls onto the ground.

Now flames lick up the corners of the bedroom and
I start to scream, for this is what I've become.

One inconsolable mass of destruction and
I burn bright.

I burn what I love without ever even trying.
Sobs like gasoline
If I cry out that I'm sorry,
We'll both end up as ashes.
So, I carry on with the rage I can never swallow and
Wail until the lack of oxygen suffocates me.
And all my possessions are up in smoke
And I collapse into a pile of brittle bones and remorse.

When the flames subside,
I am nothing but a stack of half-truths and cinder.
Ash-filled lungs cough up apologies and
I know if I keep doing this, there will cease to be anyone
to apologize to.
Who keeps a ball of fire around as a compatriot?
A lover?
A daughter?

So, I weep, until my tears clear enough of my face that my
remains can be identified once again.
My mother will offer me a drink I don't deserve and
suggest I continue to chase after the sleep that always
eludes me.
And I'll start again.
Broken down and fragile, only half alive
Like a pile of kindling.

Corpus Delicti

In dark wild forests, when a mother gives birth to her young she will
Eat the placenta and remaining tissue after delivery.
This is so nearby predators do not smell the fresh blood
and know there is offspring to prey upon.

She erases the evidence of birth to protect her babies.
No body,
No prey,
No crime.

Man is cruel in a way animals cannot be.
For when a wolf seeks out a fawn he is hunting for a meal
and will generously kill his prey
Before consuming the corpse.
Leaving behind only what he cannot digest.
No more body,
No more prey,
No crime.

Yet you hunted me for sport.
Lured me into capture with the promise of love

And reveled in my torture like that alone was enough to sustain you.
My butchered body,
Me, your domesticated prey.
You pushed upon me the guilt of all
Your crimes.

Where is my carcass?
For when I feel the flesh attached to my body I know it is not my own.
What did you do to me?
Did you take trophies to mimic a hunter?
All you are is a plague.

Where are my eyes?
The ones that contained galaxies,
Not the dull counterfeit gaze reflected back to me in the mirror.
How did you dispose of my lips?
Did you sew them shut thinking that would keep me silent?

I am no man's prey, though you treated me lower than a beast.
Maybe I am an animal now.
A raw and feral thing.
After savagely gnawing off my ankle you kept me shackled by
Swallowing my screams under flickering yellow lights,
I limped away from you inch by inch.

Blood on your hands wasn't enough for a bastard such as yourself.

I had stained the linoleum kitchen flooring as I clawed my way out of hell.

Leaving a trail that can never be scrubbed away.

I will never be your prey.

As surely as you will never evade punishment for your crimes

Now tell me,

Where is my body?

Girls! Girls! Girls!

Girls! Girls! Girls!
Girls for sale! Girls for consumption!
We have girls dissected,
Girls bisected,
Girls by the pound!

Girls here!
We have every kind you could desire!
Blondes, brunettes, redheads,
Skinny fingers
Red lips
Huge tits
Girls for rent! Girls by the hour!
Girls that can't say no,
Girls that can't say anything!

Gorgeous girls!
Fresh Girls!
Barely legal!
We'll throw in a skirt you can slide your hand up for an
additional $20,
Pay a little extra and you can get

Smiles! Smiles! Smiles!

Girls! Real Girls!
Girls in alleyways
Girls stuffed in closets
Girls on surgical tables
Girls getting liposuction as a high school graduation present!

No women, never women.

Women have jobs,
And dreams,
And people who love them.
Women aren't fun, you can't wrap your fist around their hair,
Or shove them down by your feet like a real doll.
Women are our coworkers. Our Sisters, Daughters, Elders.
Women can't bend to your faceless fantasies.

That's why here we sell Girls!
Girls here for a fun time!
Girls here for you to use as you please!
Compliant,
Disposable,
Subhuman.
Girls! Girls! Girls!

Use them

Abuse them

Throw their battered corpses out of your pickup truck window like a cigarette once you're finished.

You won't be satisfied with just one!

No cards, just cash!
No names, just fun!
Just men being men with our
Girls! Girls! Girls!

Heirlooms and Empty Rooms

For someone who is hardly ever truly alone,
I am
Morbidly lonely.

Oftentimes my presence seems to be as noteworthy as the
furniture lining the walls of an oversized room.
One made for social gatherings yet the only thing it's
gathered as of late is dust and flat,
Hollow promises of a hypothetical future event.

This is just as well, for I feel as if my purpose is equal to
the
Frozen hands of the clock mounted crookedly above a door
frame.

If I weren't so full of Nothing perhaps I would feel
embarrassment flood over my chest.
Or the inclination to go out and engage in conversations
instead of merely participating in the narrative.

The scar is not the wound.

I think of my sister.
I think of her small pristine hands and sunset eyes.
When she intertwines her fingers with her boyfriend's I am reminded
There are moments in time I am not a part of.

I whisper goodnight to my mother before slipping into my bedroom.
I don't know if she hears me, I don't know if my farewell is meant to benefit her or myself.

I am at home in my isolation,
I find myself uneasy when happy for too many consecutive moments.
I am afraid if I speak up, everything will spill out at once and I will lose grip of the one possession that I know to be authentic.
Loneliness is a family heirloom.

OCD and Me

It's been so long! How are you doing?

Well,
you're seeing me dressed in sweatpants and a jacket that's
just nice enough to seem like I've been in lounge wear all
afternoon instead of waking up fifteen minutes ago and
slumping out of bed because I couldn't hold my bladder
any longer and I put my hair up in a ponytail so I look like
there's been an actual amount of effort put towards my
appearance when in reality I've been compulsively
scratching the back of my head and neck to the point where
sores have started to form you're right I do look fresh and
yes I did wash my face four times because I awoke to find
a pimple on my right cheek the same side of my face that
bears the scar from when I had a seizure in the garage and
fell face down onto the three splintering homemade
wooden steps leading into the house and after aggressively
popping the pimple until nothing but blood will flow from
the abused pore the surrounding skin rubbed off rather
easily I scrubbed my face raw because my mind keeps
playing the same images of maggots festering under my
skin on repeat and now the image of fresh eggs being laid

into the open flesh is seared into my gray matter and I am so sorry I haven't offered you a seat yet please take the one with the back facing towards the window I'll say it's because I'm concerned the sun will get in your eyes and cause an annoyance but really it's because I need the chair with its back facing the wall so I know no one can come up behind me and choke me in my own home not that I think anyone would do that but people have vandalized our mailbox repeatedly and really am I worth more than a mailbox if I can't even shower without music blasting in the bathroom that way I don't need to focus on touching my skin the skin on the body that is damaged beyond repair but if I spend one hundred dollars on a designer perfume then maybe I can play pretend long enough to get dressed but I don't want any clothing to be fitted closely enough to give my figure any definition I would rather be sexless and wrapped in oversized polyester so I can rub the hem on the sleeves until they're threadbare because that's better than rubbing holes in my skin like the colonies of sores living on the back of my head I need them to heal although if I feel skin flakes due to my flesh healing I will vomit and then I'll be so disgusted with myself that I'll brush my teeth until my gums bleed and watch the red slink down the faucet drain it matches the blood coming from the pimple I just popped on my face that I will soak in astringent and maybe bleach if I can touch the bottle without thinking about how many dead skin cells are resting on its plastic handle the filthy bottle of an unforgiving all-purpose cleanser now that's an oxymoron if there ever was one I'll put anything on this repulsive spot of skin where I got a pimple because I'm certain that a maggot is moving as we sit here breathing.

I'm feeling great! How are you?

Missed Connection

To say I never loved you is a lie.
You were springtime, sunlight.
Soft and sweet and nearly bursting with potential.

On days when the earth beneath my feet is spinning,
Where I feel as though I'm wearing a stranger's skin and
I'm watching my life through a piece of cellophane,

I remember your birthday.

I lie in my parents' bed, staring at the ceiling in the early
afternoon.
Trying to replicate human touch without compromising
my body.

I close my eyes and try to count the freckles that adorned
your nose and disappeared into your hairline.
It was too easy to leave. Do you ever think of me?

I know your favorite color.

I did everything right.

I smiled.

I spoke softly.

I allowed myself to be crushed into pieces smaller than sand.

What happened?

Waiting

There is colored chalk scribbled on the sidewalk.
How long have the neighbors been children?
How long does childhood last?
I can't remember my own.
I don't need a fortune teller to show me how I will die,
I already know.
Waiting.

Waiting is a merciless killer, masquerading as a necessity.
A formality.
Patience.

It flows steadily out of air vents
Wraps around my larynx. My throat quivers with the
added weight.
Swirls and dissipates around the room like an exhale of
smoke.
It squeezes my sides more tightly than you ever could.

A python is lying in the center of the room and
I am the only one who sees it.

It would be rude to interrupt the conversation, so its presence goes without mention.
I find myself waiting.

This reptile slinks towards me and
Now I am frantically glancing across the room,
Desperate for eye contact or acknowledgment from the people lining the walls.

But it isn't my turn to speak, so I wait.

A man with a shiny badge upon his breast has the floor,
people are entranced by his wit and humor.
What was so funny?
I couldn't hear.

I wait as the beast makes itself comfortable around my ankles. He shows no indication of stopping.

I'm desperate to shout out for help, but the man in a poorly fitted suit is in the middle of a tired anecdote,
So, I wait.

Can you see the cracks in my smile?
The vein twitching under my eye?
While I've been holding my tongue the python shows what I swear is a smirk as he slithers up the length of my leg,
Bursting
Capillaries as it now rests snugly upon my waist.

I speak up now.
Exclaiming that people must acknowledge this imminent danger. As the party slowly turns in my direction, I receive an assortment of reactions, from annoyance to amusement. The host in his dark robes is not pleased by my outburst.

A man with a baton suggests I should get a drink.
Perhaps I am overwhelmed and simply imagining
The coiling around my middle, halting the flow of blood to my legs.
I do not dare to dismiss the advice of a man with a gun on display.

I do not miss the twisted smirk sent my way from the man across the room
In silver bracelets.
I shiver.
In this moment we are both chained to the floor,
Waiting.

I am frozen in my spot as discourse flows again like smooth vermouth.
A far more appealing poison than the one I am being taunted with.
I close my eyes and exhale as the
Snake surrounds my trembling shoulders,
It is almost my turn to speak.

The silent serpent flicks his tongue against my earlobe.
Dejected,
I resign myself to being his dinner. Whilst it crushes my
ribs I swallow my screams to make my suffering more
Digestible as I prepare to be digested.

It is only after I collapse,
My face swollen purple,
Blue lips hidden under red cosmetics and lids draped over
bloodshot eyes, that people begin to turn and take notice.
Immediately, someone crouches over and peels back my
eyelid to shine a flashlight
There is no response.

Why didn't I speak up when I had the chance?
Why did I wait so long? What was I thinking?
I must have been
Demented, choosing
To wait so long for assistance.

At least my corpse will be convenient to dispose of.
This, they will do quickly.
After a voice can no longer speak up,
There is no purpose in
Waiting.

Heatwave

That's how it goes, isn't it?
The scar will pucker and twist along my skin and brand me
with white-hot regret for years.
Long after you've left.
After I've been told to not spend any more time thinking
about it.
Like the words you spoke aren't tattooed across a
trembling canvas.
Passersby act like they aren't visible.
Like I don't remember how you promised to give me a
child
When I was a child myself.

Don't touch me.
Don't you dare think these were just words.
I opened a vein when you opened your zipper.
And now you're gone.
And I am like an experiment gone awry.
Half barely constructed, half slowly falling apart.
Like the bottoms on a pair of shoes that have
Melted onto the asphalt in this damn heatwave.

I feel your shadow creep up the length of my leg, and I wonder,
If I chop off the hand, will two grow back?
Then I remember it's over.
I turn on my side while cold sweat runs down my neck.
It's over.
You're gone.
And I am left where I started:
Alone,
Overheated,
And covered in scars.

Delicate Flower

I cut my foot.
Or rather, I have a cut on my foot.
I'm not sure how I received the wound, but it stares back
at me regardless.

It's not deep enough to bleed;
Just a scrape of irritated reddish-purple running across a
thin canvas.
A reminder that injury is constant even once the urge to
inflict has diminished.

I wonder what the teenage version of myself thinks of me
now.
A self that could look at me now and see what her actions
led to.
"I didn't mean to, I had no idea," she would say.
"I know," I would tell her,
But I don't know if I forgive myself yet.

I am my mother's daughter, but not the only one.

Last summer, my mother told me of a woman who had entered her place of work and each of her daughters shared a name with a different type of flower.
A family garden.

What type of flower am I?
I'd like to pretend I could be a pansy. Something soft and sweet and small,
Something I know I will never be.
I imagine my sister as a marigold.
Bold and proud and bright.
Not only a beauty, but helpful in a garden.

No, I am not soft like a pansy.
Nor am I a beautiful, helpful marigold.
If I were to be a flower, my best approximation would be a rose.
Classic.
Expected.
And therefore, easy to overlook.
Even if I could be as glamorous as a rose, my thorns would prick those who touch me indiscriminately.

Not deeply enough to bleed, but a reminder that injury is constant.
Even once the urge to inflict has diminished.

If

If I saw him
If I sat down across from the man who took everything
From a ghost of a girl,
I would bring a cotton wipe.

I wouldn't speak, not at first.
He doesn't deserve the comfort of conversation.
Hoping he would suffocate in the silence,
I would take my cotton wipe, blank and sterile
And stain it with eyeliner and mascara.

I would rub off any cosmetic buffer I might have applied.
Red and raw, he would have to look at me.

He would have to see how I wear my sadness on my
complexion.
It's sprinkled in amongst the freckles on the bridge of my
nose,
The creases near my lips, the furrow of my brow.

He would see the panic and grief that darkened the delicate
skin

Under my eyes.

Eyes that have been bloodshot, hazy and weary from keeping guard
Of my bedroom window for six years.
Ensuring that no monsters could crawl into my room or slither under my bed.

I would sit there, my skin on display for as long as necessary.
I would make him see every pore, line, and eyelash.
My face as bare as the body he once took pleasure in violating.

If I saw him, I would make him see me.

He might not know who I am, not at first.
He might not be able to recognize the skeleton from his closet
Might not be able to identify my remains from the others in the mass grave he has created.

Do I look different?
Far removed from the soft trembling girl
Who now lives a Woman with a razor tongue.
A Woman who bites the heads off snakes.
Do I look pretty?
I had my braces removed.

If I saw him
In handcuffs like the ones, he'd fantasized about placing
on me,
I wouldn't cry.
I wouldn't offer a smile,
Something so seemingly limited in supply.
He doesn't deserve to see the grin I've worked so hard to
create.

I would simply stare at him.
Match Evil's gaze and refuse to blink first.
I want him to look at me,
To notice my imperfections and understand that
This is the face that has ensured from this day on,
He will never know peace.

This is the profile of a woman who rose out of darkness
To guarantee he will never again be able to destroy another
life.

If I saw him
I would lean in on my elbows, closer to my personal
carcinogen.
I would steal his last moment as a free man
The way a teenager steals their parents' cigarettes.
Exhale the smoke while I stare straight ahead.

I would glare at him until he had no choice but to
memorize my features.

The face that will remind him every day how abhorrently repulsive
He truly is.
The face that will flash behind his eyelids when trying to sleep
And escape the living hell he created.

He will know my name.
He will know who I am.
I am Elizabeth Goddamn Green.

If I saw him again,
He would see me.

Rescheduled

Did you think you could slip away,
Slither on your yellow belly between the grimy bars and
leave?
Beg, cry out to the nearest officer that you have children
at home, and you must get back to them?

Did you mention the bruised child stuffed underneath your
mattress?
Stained ivory that cannot simply be cleaned away.
The blonde in the freezer,
The freckled brunette in the garden,
The one with her braces still on tied up downstairs,
How about the redhead hanging in the storage unit?
You told me all the time how red was your favorite.

Or did you just claim the two you keep pictures of in the
folder on your phone that doesn't require a password?

You are not the victim.

I hope you understand that.
When I allow myself to hope, that is what I wish for.

I need you to know you were digging your own grave
when you threw me inside that ditch.
Another body disposed of.

I don't care how long it takes for me to crawl out.
It's been seven years already and there is not a second that
passes
Where I am not
Climbing,
Cursing,
Clawing
Inch by inch out of this grave.

I'll work through the cold.
The hazy slurries of mud and snow that blind my vision.
I'll work through the rain that threatens my grip.
I'll work while the sun scorches my back and leaves me
with blisters.
Paradisiacal caresses compared to the thought of your
touch.

Dates can change.
Matters are delayed for a myriad of reasons.
But every time you close your eyes, know this:
I am one inch closer to you,
One signed document ahead of you,
One impact statement to the side of you,
And Hell will follow with every step I take.

Nothing

I listened to breakup songs for months after being
interviewed.
Pretending those sparkling, algorithmic chart toppers were
all that had happened.

I insisted that I was experiencing
Heart break that could be mended with a key change and
ice cream.
Food held no flavor, a chilled scoop of chocolate swirl was
A mouthful of ashes.
Stubbed out his cigarette on my tongue.

So full of Nothing,
I had no room to experience what had happened.

Murderers are charged with homicide.
Pyromaniacs with arson.
Addicts with possession.

He faces no penalty for what he has done.

Charges have been filed, of course.
For solicitation, for possession.
For keeping trophies.
For the physical remnants of the aftermath.
Yet nothing for the destruction of a child.

Nothing for the dismemberment of my psyche,
For the blood that has been spilt from my wrists.
The blood that dribbles from my mouth every time I must
reaffirm a detail regarding his malicious transgressions.

Nothing,
For the blood he fantasized about.
The innocence gushing from the wound of the jagged knife
he wished to penetrate my thigh with.
Before penetrating the gash, himself.
Shock and betrayal oozing over the comforter and seeping
onto coarse carpet.

Nothing,
For the nightmares broadcasted beneath my eyelids when
I feel that I might be able to loosen my grip on control long
enough to rest.

Nothing,
For the seizures he assists in orchestrating.
I am nothing but a marionette convulsing on the ground,
writhing from the strings he pulls even now from a
distance.

These damned performances reminding me
I am not the captain of my ship, as I am not even the
commander of my limbs.

While I gasp and choke and my eyelids flutter, he sleeps
soundly without remembering my name.
He eats freely, while I vomit from the thought of him
approaching my window.

He is afforded free counsel and will work out a plea
When
I,
For seven years,
Would plea every night this would be the evening I would
not awake from.

He will be sentenced at the court's discretion,
To related charges that occurred around my torture.
But for my suffering, he and I will receive the same.
Nothing.

Can I Be Finished?

Every piece I write sounds exactly alike.
All different colors of the same dress.
The one I wear to funerals.
This song has been played one too many times and now,
My mind skips over the melody in wait of something new.

My emotions are processed and mass manufactured.
These tears are recycled and can be bought on clearance.
I bleed on command as I rip off layers
Of skin in hope of finding something original.

Something to prove I'm still worth your attention.
If no one is looking,
I'm not sure if I exist.
Tell me what to say,
To get you to linger in the
Doorway for just a moment longer.
Before I'm left with the body I no longer recognize.
The thoughts I refuse to claim as my own.

I'll schedule my hysterics for a matinée if that works better for you.
When I stop screaming,
Sobbing,
Shaking in my bed at night,
Will you still remember my existence?
Or am I only fun to look at when I'm in pieces, like a mosaic?

Messy

Never trust a Man whose house is messy.

Not messy
In the way of a crumpled blanket lying on the floor, or a
pizza box casually tossed aside.
Messy
Like you're entering the cave of a predator and there are
miscellaneous bones lining the entranceway,
A dismembered hand with an emerald ring still attached to
its phalange.

Filthy
As in being invited to enter a sparkling bright kitchen with
a child's lock on the medicine cabinet.
You know the only person affected by this lock is a woman
too weak to walk the length of the hallway, let alone fight
against plastic clamps.

Begrimed
Like the freshly washed bed sheets meticulously stacked
in the linen closet

While the bed he has banished a dying woman to remains unmade.
Irreversible stains bleed into the fabric, yet the
Man feigns ignorance and locks the door to a bedroom that is without windows.

Clear glass panels show a child sitting alone outside, escaping into a world of fantasy.
This is not a singular experience.
The child has become an expert at raising herself despite the numerous adults living in her house.
You can tell by the blood encrusted underneath the Man's fingernails.

Tarnished like the freshly sanitized bank account he checked upon that morning.
The pristine car he drives to meet his mistress.
The immaculate computer he spends endless hours using, for work, of course.

Do not trust a man who lives in divine purity while allowing his supposed loved ones to survive in squalor.
For he is as deceptive as a siren.
Luring you in under the disguise of
Glamor,
Anticipating your final breath.

A wretched creature,
The Man

Has convinced his neighbors that his house is polished and
glowing.
They shower him in
Praise for being an excellent provider.
In reality he
Syphons resources from the home like a
Parasite.
How gratifying it would be,
To watch his teeth, fall out
One
By
One
Until he is unable to latch onto the neck of his next host.

Never trust a man whose house is messy,
Its glimmering, sterile façade is the easiest way to catch a
glimpse into
His slimy, repugnant soul.

A mess in every sense of the word.

The Big Reveal

Every courthouse tastes the same.
Metallic.
Like the clotted liquid sitting in my throat.
I examine the hallway and wonder if any of these sharks
can smell the dribble of blood
That has seeped into their exhibit.
My tissue balled up in a trembling fist.

The rehearsed platitudes directed toward me fade into
static as my gaze is captured by
Armed men whose appearances resemble toy soldiers.
Then I saw him.

He looked so
Human.
His eyes cast downwards; spine ridged.
Seven years of silence have brought me
Seven yards away from the creature who treated my body
like a marionette.
All I see is a Man.

My mind had written him too well.

Where are his fangs?
His scales, his claws?
The forked tongue that whispered so softly in my ear.
The voice that convinced me to take a bite of
Forbidden fruit,
Its plump, juicy flesh actually
A baited hook. Piercing through my cheek?

My heart has yet to palpitate,
No scream escapes my lips
My eyes as dry as the stale air standing stagnant in this
building.
Silence as his figure slouches
And seeks refuge behind the desk of his attorney.

Where is the Man that hid behind a keyboard?
The Butcher who complimented my body while running a
knife across his tongue,
Planning how to best carve me open for his consumption.
The one who slid a noose around my neck and assured me
it would soon be replaced with a ring on my finger.
Where is the monster?

Not once did he dare turn to meet my gaze.
No, he faced forward.
Shifting uncomfortably in a cheap,
Ill-fitting suit.
No mask, no costume
Only skin, dampened with droplets of perspiration

And
Hands placed upon the desk for all to monitor
It all looked so sadistic, yet innocent.
So distressingly normal.

All I saw was a Man,
One indistinguishable from the men we pass on the street,
Invite into our homes,
Trust to raise our children.

Now the present has sunk in,
I can see things clearly.
All I saw was a Man,
That's all that monster ever was.

Not All Men

Not all men become defense attorneys.
Slender as a weeping willow's branch,
Purposely passive, poisonous manipulations wafting past
their coffee-stained teeth
With some type of *faux* animal skin stitched onto the
elbows of their blazer,
No, not all men become defense attorneys
But some do.

Not all attorneys call a haunted fifteen-year-old a
Woman.
An inescapable temptress,
A fifteen-year-old
Woman
Who forced a defenseless forty-two-year-old man to fall in
Love
With her.
Leaving no option but to devour her slowly,
Hacking off one limb at a time.
Relishing the screams and sobs and shed tears.

Not all attorneys stand before a judge and explain that the fifteen-year-old
Woman
All but begged a man older than her mother to rip away her humanity,
Layer by layer, like the wrapping paper of the most coveted present under the Christmas tree.

Not all attorneys suggest that a year of grotesque abuse and stalking is
Love.
That a blood-soaked letter
Written in code,
Signed under an alias and
Sent to a child's high school with no return address is a sign of
Adoration. Of concern.
But some do.

Not all men become judges.
Arriving late to his single case of the day,
Glancing at the clock repeatedly while a scarred survivor gives an impact statement that took seven years to finish
But some do.

Not all judges sympathize with a pedophile by explaining that
He gets it, he has children of his own.
A family man.

Not all judges smile at the defense like two good ole boys,
Old pals who plan on cracking open a couple of bottles
later.
The same way that monster cracked open my rib cage.

No, not all judges state aloud that they don't believe a child
predator would
Benefit from prison time and
Dismiss the option immediately.
But some do.

Not all judges mindlessly parrot the scathing words of the
defense and agree
It is unfortunate such a fine, upstanding man fell in
Love
With a child.
This poor predator needs therapy, rehabilitation,
Not condemnation.

Not all judges tell a newly constructed, cautiously sewn
together
Woman
To leave the past behind already,
To stop playing the victim during their day in court.

Droplets of self-righteous bile trickle down the painfully
plain white walls

Due to the amount of condescending condensation that leaves his mouth.
Pious air thick enough to suffocate any protests.
No,
No.
Not all judges
Not all attorneys
Not all men.

Walking on Eggshells

An 'Eggshell Victim'
Is that the legal term?
When referring to a teenager who found comfort in chaos
and control with a razor blade?

The entrapment and self-hatred stripped scarlet across my
clavicles as I smeared on tacky lip gloss and agreed to
become the contemptuous consumer's plaything.

Let my sickly sweating body be sufficient sacrifice.
I'll lay still. Stiffly spread open on a platter,
Silently upon the sterile steel of a butchering table,
Motionless and tied to the legs.

Anything so that those serrated canines stay focused on
me.
Anything to allow the others a chance to escape the stare
of the beast.

To volunteer myself for slaughter,
To lock myself in the occupied cage and close the curtains.
To smile until the muscles in my face have no meaning.

To hand over my parachute as I take my step off the plane.

I stood atop the gates of hell to keep the attention of this monster.
Weathered shoes connecting toe to heel,
I wobbled across crumbling stone with a
Razor-sharp edge,
Thinner than any tightrope
To spare other children from his searing hot touch.

I sang until my lungs burst,
Danced until my feet bled,
Pitched prose until no sound could emanate from these shredded vocal cords.
Half dead and panting, waiting to repeat the routine.

And I am the one being compared to the fragile shell of an egg?

Not the serpent?
The coward who could not meet my gaze.
The gutless lowlife who is so petrified by women that he must butcher a child and rip out her spine,
Twisting until each vertebra shatter.
Watching them drop to the floor
One by one
To feel control?

How rich a comparison,

Coming from the man who views the world atop the throne of a false God.

The man who never sees the butchered remains of his sentencing.

The type of man who can say this with such disregard is

A man who has never been cracked.

An Honor with no honor.

Fair

It continues on,
The war.
A war that has lived longer than the soldiers fighting her.
And I am called to stand at attention before the general.

Overnight I have transformed from the adolescent powder
keg that ignited this battle to the right hand of the General
herself.

The enemy side has raised a flag.
Tattered and filthy, but still recognizable as white.
I am volunteered to cross over enemy lines and discuss the
particular benefits that come with surrender.

My feet are heavy.
Steps uneven.
Each feels as if I am bound to metal chains that drag over
the battlefield and ring out sounds of exhaustion and guilt.

The synthetic grins I receive upon entry are painted on, yet
I am not affected by the opposing leadership.
For I know I am about to dine with a cannibal.

Settling in the splintered chair,
I think I might laugh at the meal presented before me.
A heart roasted upon a spit.
Just like the one that had been clawed out of my chest all those years ago.

I smooth out my napkin as legal jargon floats past my ears and falls onto the dirt.
Straightening my spine, I stare at the man I am to be negotiating with.
The one who left me for dead.
Bleeding out,
Gasping for air that couldn't be inhaled quickly enough.

The silver scar tissue that extends down my leg tightens and stings, but I do not look away from the man opposite me.
One should always be observant when dining with such a man.
He has already robbed me of one body and I cannot locate her bones.
Perhaps he tossed them to the dogs.

Other men situate themselves on each side of him and ask me if I agree to their terms of surrender.
I find myself in a loathsome position.
One where I must decide if the punishment the monster has selected for himself is fair.

Fair.

Fair,
When blades pierced my skin for his entertainment and arousal.
When I wrapped my arms around my ribs at night to hold in the screams while waves of grief and terror ran through my body.

The muscles of my back would seize in irritation as
I glanced at the alarm clock to see how many minutes
I had left to mourn my slaughtered innocence before washing my face to prepare for school.

Fair,
Whenever I see his face in a crowd and duck down as if I were in the trenches. Mud and tears splattered over my face as I freeze.
And the only difference between the frozen corpse lying stiff in those trenches and
Myself is that eventually I will have to stand up and continue to walk through hell.

Fair,
They are asking the soldier to forgive the bullet lodged in flesh,
Still bleeding and shake the hand of the marksman.

This is not fair. This is not justice.

This plea is only a recognition of error. There has been no apology given, no reparations disbursed.

Does he think I am to share his guilt?

That I am to accept my role in his destruction of my innocence because I was too petrified to stop him?

I will never sign a document that concedes any benefits to the man who both stole my adolescence and poisons my adulthood.

This contract is saturated with the blood of every girl who came before me.

I will never express empathy towards that creature.

Teeth like serrated knives.

A pound of flesh missing from my thigh.

I will never forget the horrors he subjected me to as they are now marked upon my skin for all to view.

I will never bring myself to forgive the man who was a hair's width away from slaughtering me entirely.

Do not ask me if his plea is fair.

Nothing is fair.

At Least

Everything I say sounds like a lie.
I speak of healing,
And it sounds like advertising for an inpatient psychiatric
program.
Maybe it is.

I swallow the anger that comes with every
'At least' thrown my way,
The platitude that strikes the side of my face so swiftly.
I raise my chin after every well-intentioned blow.
"At least it's over"
"At least it wasn't too bad"
They see my bared teeth and assume it's a smile
Lips stretched as thin as my patience.

"At least it's over"
For them.
It's over for them.
The woman who spreads gossip like bird seed, it's over for
her.
The hungry suburban scavengers who come to peck out of
her hand,

It's over for them.

I stay silent,
I don't correct them
For flames dance upon my tongue and
I want to scream.
I would burn this entire town to ashes.
The only remnant being a child's nearly melted plastic doll
lying at my feet.
Half smiling, one eye remaining.

I would
Destroy every part of myself
Again
To believe that
At least it wasn't too bad,
At least it's over,
At least.

What a Joke

I never understood why I do
I just do. I still do.
If something catches my attention whilst wandering
through the store,
I must touch the object with both hands
To make it even.

At midnight I pace back and forth.
Wearing a path into the carpet
As I practice the correct way to say hello:
Hold eye contact for three seconds
Then find relief staring at their mud-caked boots.

Every summer
Tears stream from the rocket's red glare
Because
A firecracker and a gunshot sound the same shooting past
my eardrums.
Sparklers are just as pretty as shrapnel, and both would
love to bury themselves under my skin.

I try

I try so very hard to get them to love me.
But with everything else, I do it incorrectly.
Spouting out every microscopic detail I've memorized about something, someone, someplace somewhere.
Only to discover my words are meaningless and off-putting halfway through.

Faces confuse me.
Sarcasm heats my ears as I fail to comprehend the joke.
I don't understand the dialogue
Flooding past my unbalanced frame, knocking me to the ground,
Palms agitated and stinging red.
But I can recognize that
This garbled string of words is intended to dismiss me.
Insult me.
To sprinkle salt on my fresh-throbbing wound and insist it's glitter.
Done so with a smile sweeter than aspartame
I understand now,
This is all a joke.
I hate that I am the punchline.

Burnout

What use is writing when there is no emotion to
orchestrate the words?
When there is no progress to report or healing to rejoice
in?

Closure is a putrid lie.
My wounds,
Gaping open,
Blood flowing down,
Pooling around the grate at the end of the street
Along with the smattering episodes of rain.

And I could compare that rain to the tears
I never shed,
Or string together some brain-dead blurb about positivity.
But what good would that do?

I could stand barefoot on the street
And demand reformation.
Scream for others to see just what has become of the little
girl once destined for success,
But there would be no echo.

For these feelings were hollow to begin with.

I am not healing.
I am furious that a scheduled appointment for my rebirth
has been jotted down in some idiotic
Clearance-priced planner next to a
Feminist quote
Manufactured in an office somewhere,
Equipped with a nepotism nursery full of exclusively male
interns.

Who benefits from me saying that everything's fine
While my world burns around me?
I have grown so tired of playing the hand I've been dealt.
I know I'm lucky,
I get to heal.
But I am infuriated that I need to in the first place.

Omnia Gratis

It's over.
I was told he pled guilty,
And I feel the same as I do throwing away expired coupons
from the junk drawer with the lid that always locks up.

There has been no release.
Nothing announced over school speakers.
There has been no confetti thrown,
Or champagne opened,
Or celebration in Times Square.

I'm not anything.
If I were anything, I could be ecstatic or miserable.
I could wallow in my trauma and sob heavily enough for
my tears to flood my parents' basement.
I could bubble over with joy and squeal and spin and shout
my elation at the stars.
If I were anything I could be numb.
I could be frozen like the fingers of a child who insisted
they didn't need to wear gloves on their walk to the bus
stop.

But I'm not anything.
I'm not nothing, that I know.
I know the ramifications of this confession.
I see the joy and excitement in the eyes of others.
I don't know how to allow myself to feel the love bestowed upon me.

The same congratulatory attention given to the winner of a beauty pageant now weighs on my head like a crown.
I've been gifted the same sash and scepter
And now the crowd is waiting to hear a speech I have not written.
I watch as the interest fades from their faces after the only thing I can think to express is a thank you.

I don't know how to feel without suffocating from my all-consuming emotions.
I always feel everything,
Maybe that's why now I feel almost nothing.

Almost Human

I always thought that I would die young.
I believed it to be a fact.
The moon reflects sunlight,
Dandelions grow in the springtime,
And I will be deceased whilst still in my youth.
I just didn't know it would happen so quickly.

As expected, I had died prematurely.
Perished silently in the night when no one was watching.
Curiously enough, I awoke the next day, and nothing
seemed to have changed.
When I spoke, people still heard me,
My sweet dog still whacked his tail against my knees.
I was offered a plate of dinner.
No one told my family they were dining with the undead.

Facing the mirror,
I prodded and pinched at the green skin and purple
splotches decorating my cadaver.
Eyed the lines inching up my wrists.
I know soon they should be filled with maggots

Angry raw skin returns my stare and I found myself too embarrassed to continue my examination.
Every movement was perfectly mimicked,
Every pantomimed expression reflected back towards me.

I walked among the living without so much as a second glance.
Watching my sister excel in every endeavor,
My brothers squabble spiritedly across the creaking wooden table.
Laying my palm across my darling boy's ribs and feeling the soft rise and fall of his breathing.

I was participating from purgatory and that was enough to dismiss any suspicion of my passing.
Who would ever suspect a death took place when the body still speaks?

It was the monster under my bed.
The bastard was efficient if anything.
He killed me quickly and quietly.
His lies were so beautiful,
His unwavering attention hypnotic.
The poison dribbling from the corner of his mouth invisible to my gaze.
And I had felt morbidly alone before his presence consumed me.

And maybe I did love him,

If only for a moment.
One moment is all it takes for life to be taken.
And he made my love feel dirty,
My admiration perverse,
My dedication pathetic and eventually lethal.

Now my love feels wrong.
And I don't know if I'll ever be able to love correctly.

I am not a phoenix,
Rising up from pitch dark ashes.
Nor am I pure enough to seek rebirth from God.
But lying here, staring at the plastic stars randomly
arranged on my ceiling,
I begin to feel almost human.

Maybe one day I'll be able to feel without drowning.
Maybe one day I will be able to tell if I am being loved
properly,
Free of sin and secrecy.
My love could be as pure as the child I once was,
And
I will live once again.

Severance

What does a woman
Want?
A new novel?
The lipstick she watched her friend reapply.
A vacation to an exotic island?
Everything that is luxurious
And coveted
And glamorous.
I want severance.

I want
My skin back.
Lathered soap runs over my body yet I am numb to the touch. Scalding hot water is not enough to rid myself of you.

I want
My eyes.
The ones that shined with all the light of the sun, blue as an open sky and once believed you when you claimed you didn't mean the pain you inflicted.

I want
My lips to be the way they were
Before you stole them.
Full and smiling, glossy
And bright.
Not the worried pout with chapped skin that has taken its
place.

I want
To be returned in mint condition,
I want
To feel human again.

I want
To be free of the cuffs that shackle my ankle to yours.
Free from the panic that creeps up the back of my neck at
the mention of you.
Free of this case that will seemingly never reach a
conclusion.

I want
To wake up and live twenty-four consecutive hours
without your existence crossing my mind.

I want severance.

I want
To walk around a grocery store without looking over my
shoulder.

I want

To enter a room without feeling the need to turn my back against the wall and count the people in attendance.

I want

To walk my dog alone in the evenings and laugh when one of my shoes lands in a puddle.

I want

To laugh.

God,

I want to laugh and squeal and snort without abandon.

Laugh until my cheeks are flushed and my face hurts from smiling,

Until I feel a warmth in my chest that I've gone years without.

I want it all without the lingering feeling that if I smile too widely you'd find me again.

I want severance.

Complete detachment from you and the poison that drips from your mouth and melts craters into the floor.

I want

Freedom from the ties that bind me to my childhood monster.

On that day, I will run faster than ever before and smell the summer air as tears run down my face.

I cannot bring myself to
Care too deeply about where you end up.
Whether that be in a penitentiary or a plastic bag.
I will find the house hate built and I will burn it to the
ground.
In the ashes, I will plant hydrangeas.
Something pink and wonderful to blossom out of corrosive
soil.

I've done my share of waiting.
I've been more patient than a saint.
My time is finally inching closer, and I know what
I want.
Severance.

Lemonade

I brushed my teeth this morning.
Gently cleansed my face,
I did not think of a single insult to hurl at my features.
I stared into the mirror and was met with the reflection of
an almost content woman, not the starving girl from years
before.

Once a savage child,
I wore my hunger like a badge of honor sewn into my skin.
As if my suffering had been the price of admission into
adulthood.
I notice the children passing by the high school.
I see the hunger in their eyes and strewn-about backpacks.

I used to think that if I prayed for forgiveness for the
actions
Done unto me by my sadist that my
Soul would heal and I could be clean once again.

Now I trace the spine of a well-worn paperback, knowing
if I can fall in love with ink and paper then surely I can fall
in love with myself.

I am not a tarnished woman.
I was never damaged to begin with.
I have become so much more than the tragedies I've suffered.

The most dangerous thing a woman can do is choose to love herself.

I am indomitable against the poison that drips from the mouths of strange men.
Viscous as a syrup I once would have found to be sickly sweet.
Rose-colored shades are now shards of broken glass lying at my feet.
Now I see in Technicolor and will not allow the world's intensity to blind me.

I painted the wall of my room yellow.
Yellow is bright and all-consuming,
It holds promises of sun-filled afternoons,
Sipping lemonade on the porch.

Closing my eyes, I run my fingers through freshly washed hair and picture the child I was.
I wish I could grasp her hand and tell her
I am whole.

In the Twilight

Autumn rain gently trickles down the gutter,
Taking along with it the early hours of the morning.
Left behind during this period of not quiet today,
I fall alongside the rain.

Falling is easy. I do it all the time.
Benzodiazepines occasionally take pity on me and grant a
dreamless sleep.
I don't want to be left alone, not with the stranger I have
become.

I cut my hair; the dark locks you claimed to love now lay
motionless on tacky, product-stained linoleum.
Feeling lighter, I glance at the asymmetric features
reflected back at me.
I am presented with a foreigner, one who shares my
shadow.
My mother compliments the change.
I do not look like my mother. I don't share her love or
grace.

For you carved me open to satisfy carnal pleasures and
now
I don't know if love or any other drug can fill the space in
my body that seems to remain permanently vacant.

Love seems so simple when it's not your own.

When love is handed out like a Valentine,
When you only need to bring enough to share with your
classmates.
Now I don't know if I have any for the strange woman
staring back at me.

Every night I gaze at the scars haphazardly disbursed
across my skin.
They have begun to turn pale
Fade into a silver that looks like a sliver of the moon.
I glance up towards the moon,
And the moon looks back down at me.
At both of me.
And it's enough.
And I am enough.

Ameliorate

I can't name the date that it started.
When I felt myself breathe again and it felt
Like I meant it.

I removed the pipe from my window.
Once again I sleep free of barricades.
Staring at the night sky my gaze is settled on the distance
between two stars.
For a moment, I live in the space between them.

I feel the wind swipe an eyelash from my cheek as I watch
my
Love trot carelessly through the changing seasons.
Four paws and one tail that never stills shred through a pile
of leaves
And warmth spreads across my chest.

Now my heart is back in my possession,
More closely resembling a porcelain figurine
Whose shattered pieces have been nudged back in place
With copious amounts of glue.

But when I clasp my hands together,
I can feel my fingers and know they belong to me.
My hair grows again, wild and frizzy yet progressing all
the same.

I am getting better.
Like the tight, pink skin found under a healing wound
I am fresh and fragile and exciting to behold.

Diamond on Display

Did you think I would remain fifteen forever?
That I would bend to your will better than a willow tree
and shake alongside its branches?

Worse yet, had your horrendous ego convinced you I was
in love?

I knew the game you reveled in before I was a moving
piece.
I had signed my agency away with ink darker than your
heart.
Did you think I would ever let you win?

You had me convinced I was ruined, one touch and I was
covered in filth dark as coal. Left to spend this life burning
alive to keep you warm.
Yet your revolting actions could not stop nature's course.

Years of pressure and heat turned me into a diamond. One
so sharp that if you dared to touch me now, I would slice
your flesh without hesitation.

You do not know me; you will never have that privilege. You will never bear witness to how I shine, how I reflect light onto others.

I know my worth without the need of an appraisal. I sparkle with more glamor than anything one could find at the jewelers.

Did you think I would allow myself to remain tossed aside?
That I would spend my days crying over you?

You may have put me through hell, but I crawled my way through on bleeding palms until I glimpsed salvation on the other side.

Did you think I would be submissive? Stay silent and resigned?

I refuse to hide myself from the world.
I am a diamond.
I'll shine
And shine
And shine.

I'm Coming Home

I have cycled through therapists like our sessions were job
interviews.
Their diagnoses acted as applications,
Each one studying my responses behind the
Comfort of a clipboard.

They spin stories out of scribbled notes,
Waxing poetic about the miracle of Forgiveness
Like it will solve all of life's maladies.
Perched behind Formica desks
They tell me to release the suffocating grip I have on my
past,
Allow that battered corpse to breathe once more.
To apply Forgiveness like a salve and this will allow my
body to heal.
I refuse.

I do not forgive that girl.
That reckless masochist.
If my body was a temple,
Then it was her fist that fractured the glass.

She never thought of consequences or healing or redemption.
Never expected to live past adolescence,
Never gave thought to a parachute before
Stepping off the plane.

No, I do not forgive the girl who
Sold my sanity by the ounce.
Who robbed me of my reflection,
The girl who abandoned my body.
White hot scar tissue runs along this hollow frame like charred wallpaper.
Fragmented bones lay in a heaping pile
A place I could never make a home.
How does one receive an apology from a girl who no longer exists?

I do not forgive, but I will wait.
Life never ceases its continual march. And
My patience for contentment, for happiness,
Is unwavering.
I've waited this long,
I'm happy to sway in the breeze
For just a while longer.

I will be tender to these old bones
And one day they will grant me a new form.
I deserve a gentle epilogue.
Until then I bide my time, waiting.

For a body that has never known me,
A body I can say is entirely mine
A body that I can make a home.

Epilogue

My name is Elizabeth Green. I was born in July of 1999, and at the time of writing this I am twenty-three years old. After the trial, my abuser was sentenced to serve one year in jail. Upon deliberating his sentence, the judge reasoned that prison "would not help [my abuser]." I have deliberately chosen not to name the pedophile who assaulted me, as I do not want his name to be associated with mine ever again. After seven years of silence, and one year of court proceedings, I am finally free. After eight years, I have decided to conclude this chapter of my life. Although the events of our lives never have a true ending, I have chosen this time to end the immense grief I have been frozen in. I am now living.

Every day I live knowing that I am not simply a victim, but a survivor. My life will forever be changed due to this experience, but I am left with a profound realization: I stood up. I stood up to a man more than twice my age, and because of this he can never hide his face. I stood up, and was pushed down, and I stood again. I have healed, and I will heal again. I decided to write these poems to let others who have been pushed down know they can and will stand again.

Resources

If you or someone you know is a victim of abuse, please contact the resources below:

National Domestic Violence Hotline: (800) 799-7233
SAMHSA's National Helpline: 1-800 662-4357
Suicide and Crisis Lifeline: 988
National Suicide Prevention Lifeline: (800) 273-8255
Crisis Text Line: 741741
Child help National Child Abuse Hotline: 1-800-422-4453

United Kingdom Resources:
Rape Crisis Centers: (0808 500 2222)
The Survivors' Trust: (0808 801 0818)
National Domestic Abuse Helpline run by Refuge (0808 200 0247)